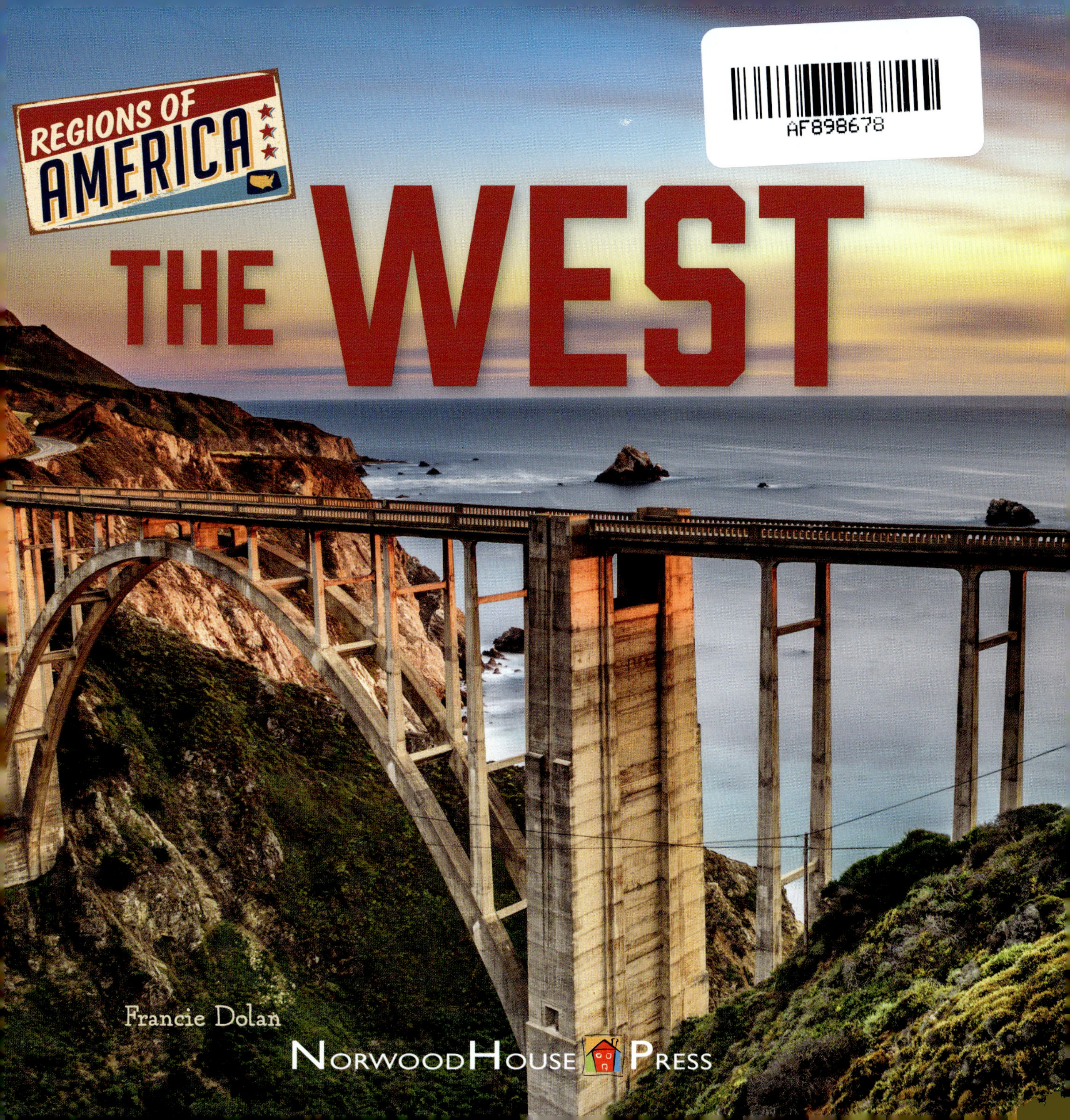

Regions of America

The West

Francie Dolan

Norwood House Press

Cataloging-in-Publication Data

Names: Dolan, Francie.
Title: The West / Francie Dolan.
Description: Buffalo, NY : Norwood House Press, 2027. | Series: Regions of America | Includes glossary and index.
Identifiers: ISBN 9781978581289 (pbk.) | ISBN 9781978581296 (library bound) | ISBN 9781978581302 (ebook)
Subjects: LCSH: Pacific States--Juvenile literature.
Classification: LCC F851.D65 2027 | DDC 979--dc23

Published in 2027 by
Norwood House Press
2544 Clinton Street
Buffalo, NY 14224

Designer: Rhea Magaro
Editor: Tricia Hoffman

Photo credits: Cover, p. 1 Nick Fox/Shutterstock.com; p. 5 Sekar B/Shutterstock.com; p. 6 Sarah Partschefeld/Shutterstock.com; p. 7 Nicholas J Klein/Shutterstock.com; p. 8 evenfh/Shutterstock.com; p. 9 Terelyuk/Shutterstock.com; p. 10 PHOTOGRAPHY IS ON/Shutterstock.com; p. 11 IM_photo/Shutterstock.com; pp. 12, 13 Library of Congress; p. 14 Richard Thornton/Shutterstock.com; p. 15 UVL/Shutterstock.com; p. 17 Valeriy Poltorak/Shutterstock.com; p. 18 Chris Allan/Shutterstock.com; p. 21 Susan Rogers/Shutterstock.com;

Printed in the United States of America

CPSIA compliance information: Batch #CSNHP27: For further information contact Norwood House Press at 1-800-237-9932.

TABLE OF CONTENTS

WHERE IS THE WEST?

The West is a **region** of the United States. It has nine states that connect to other U.S. states. It also includes Alaska and Hawaii. They are in different parts of the world.

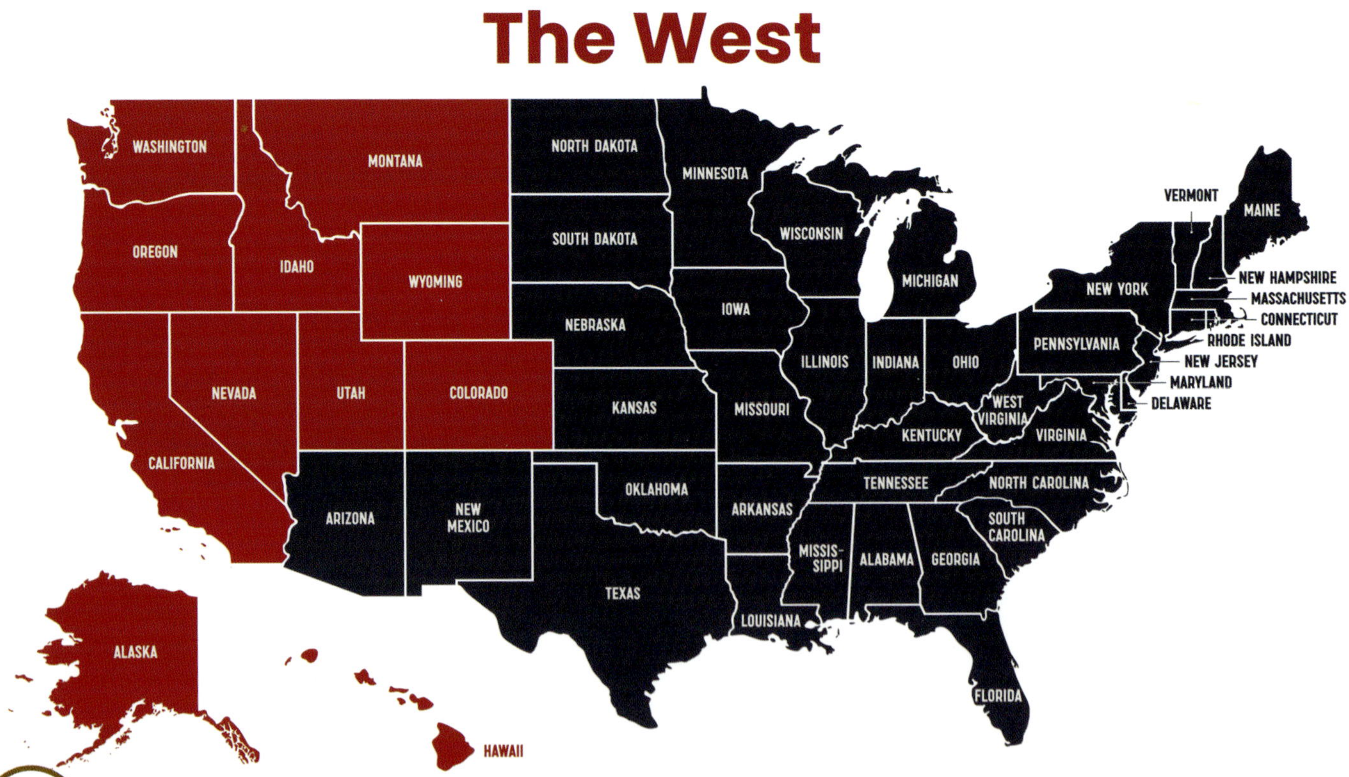

THE LAND

The West begins near the Rocky Mountains. It borders Canada in the north. It stretches all the way to the Pacific Ocean.

Some places in the West are **temperate**.

Some are **arid**.

Alaska is in the far northwestern corner of North America. It has the most land of any U.S. state. Mount McKinley is here. It is the highest peak on the continent.

Eight major islands form Hawaii. They are in the middle of the Pacific Ocean. It is warm and **tropical** there all year.

The West has many different **ecosystems**. The giant Mojave Desert covers parts of California, Nevada, and Utah.

Oregon and Washington have rainforests with giant trees.

The Great Plains stretch across parts of Montana, Wyoming, and Colorado.

THE PEOPLE

Indigenous people once lived across the region. Some tribes were the Shoshone and Chumash.

In the 1800s, **pioneers** traveled across the continent to settle the West. They came in wagons pulled by horses. Many went to California to look for gold.

Today, many people live in small towns. Some work on farms, ranches, and ski resorts.

Many people live in **urban** areas. Los Angeles, California, is the second largest city in America.

THINGS TO SEE AND DO

In Washington, you can hike to the **crater** rim of Mount St. Helens. This volcano had a giant eruption in 1980.

You can learn to surf in Huntington Beach, California. Its nickname is Surf City, U.S.A.

You can watch Old Faithful erupt in Yellowstone National Park. This **geyser** is in Wyoming. Every 90 minutes or so, it shoots boiling water into the sky.

GLOSSARY

arid (AR-id): extremely dry because of a lack of rain

crater (KRAY-tur): the mouth of a volcano

ecosystems (EE-koh-sis-tuhmz): natural communities where plants, animals, and their environment all work together

geyser (GYE-zur): an underground hot spring that shoots boiling water and steam into the air

Indigenous (in-DI-juh-nuhs): the earliest known people to live in a place

pioneers (pye-uh-NEERZ): people who explore unknown territories and settle there

region (REE-juhn): an area or territory; part of a country

temperate (TEM-pur-it): having temperatures that are rarely very high or very low

tropical (TRAH-pi-kuhl): having to do with regions of the world that are always hot and rainy

urban (UR-buhn): having to do with cities and city life

THINKING QUESTIONS

1. Name three states in the West.
2. What Western states touch the Pacific Ocean?
3. Name a big city in the West.
4. Name one Native American tribe from the West.
5. What is Mount St. Helens?

INDEX

ABOUT THE AUTHOR

Francie Dolan is a writer from Seattle, Washington. She loves American history and trivia. It is her goal to travel to all 50 states, visit their capital cities, and eat a special food from each place.